THE
MIDDLE AGES

Written by Dr Sarah McNeill

ACKNOWLEDGMENTS

Illustrated by
Julian Baker
Chris Forcey
Steve Longden
Roger Payne
Tony Smith
Stephen Sweet
Andrew Wheatcroft

Picture credits
Front cover: Top – Detail from "Très Riches Heures du Duc de Berry" Mars, chateau de Lusignan by Pol de Limbourg; Chantilly/Musée Condé/Photographie Giraudon. **Bottom left** – Detail from "View of Paris from Froissart's Chronicles"; The British Library.

Edited by
Julia Roles

Designed by
Simon Borrough

Published in 1998 by
Macdonald Young Books
an imprint of Wayland Publishers Limited
61 Western Road
Hove
East Sussex BN3 1JD

You can find Macdonald Young Books on the internet at
http://www.wayland.co.uk

Devised and produced by
Andromeda Oxford Limited
11-15 The Vineyard
Abingdon
Oxfordshire OX14 3PX
England

Copyright © 1998 Andromeda Oxford Limited

ISBN 0-7500-2429-1
Printed in Italy by Vallardi, Milan

CONTENTS

INTRODUCTION

The Middle Ages lasted for about 1,000 years. Although historians sometimes argue about dates, it is generally agreed that the Middle Ages began when the last Roman emperor lost power in the West, in 476, and that they ended sometime between 1400 and 1450. We call this period 'medieval'. All across Europe there are signs of the medieval past. Cathedrals tell us of the stunning artistic and engineering skills people had, and of their great belief in God. Castles tell us about the power of the nobles. Many of our towns and villages were founded in the Middle Ages. Our landscape was shaped by peasants who cleared forests and brought new land into cultivation. Modern political units like the nations of France, England and Scotland took shape at this time. In all these ways, the world built then survives today.

VISITING MUSEUMS

You will be able to find pictures and objects made in the Middle Ages, like the ones in this book, in museums all over the world.

HOW TO USE THIS BOOK

This book explores and explains the world of the Middle Ages. Each double-page spread looks at a particular aspect of life in medieval times, building up a fascinating picture of medieval civilization.

HEADING

The subject matter of each spread is clearly identified by a heading prominently displayed in the top left-hand corner.

INTRODUCTION

Concise yet highly informative, this text introduces the reader to the topics covered in the spread. This broad coverage is complemented by more detailed exploration of particular points in the numerous captions.

SPOTLIGHTS

A series of illustrations at the bottom of each page encourages the reader to look out for objects from the Middle Ages that can be found in museums.

CASTLES

Castles belonge and knights – the people in the land sign that the own both in times of w Castles were home holds at the same ti designed to be diffic enemy to attack. Th were built in the 9th centuries, from earth Designs gradually cha up with new fighting r

MOTTE AND BAILEY CASTLE

Motte and bailey castles were built in the 11th and 12th centuries. The bailey was an enclosed yard with buildings inside. The motte was a mound of earth with a timber tower on top.

LOOK OUT FOR THESE

SPIRAL STAIRCASE
Spiral staircases were designed so that a right-handed invader, fighting his way in, would hit the stonework if he used his sword.

16

INSET ARTWORKS

Subjects that help to explain particular points are shown as insets along with an explanation of their significance.

DETAILED INFORMATION

From the building of their magnificent cathedrals to the everyday life of nobles and peasants, the reader is given a wealth of information to help understand medieval people.

ILLUSTRATIONS

High-quality, full-colour artwork brings the world of the Middle Ages to life. Each spread is packed with visual information.

REFERENCE TAB

Each group of subjects is keyed with a special colour to the contents page of the book so that different sections can be found quickly and easily.

GREAT TOWER
From the 11th century, great stone towers were built. They were called 'keeps'. Attackers could not burn down a stone keep.

SQUARE CORNERS
Early castles had square corners. But these could be weakened by tunnelling underneath and made the flat walls an easy target to hit with rocks – hence round turrets developed.

NARROW SLIT WINDOWS
Windows were narrow on the outside, to keep out missiles fired by the enemy. Inside, they broadened out to give an archer room to fire on his attackers.

THICK WALLS
Stone castles had massive walls. Some were 4.5 to 6 metres (15 to 20 feet) thick.

BUTTRESSES
Buttresses were used to give the walls even greater strength.

FORE BUILDING
To make attack difficult, there was no way in at ground level. Entry was through the fore building, higher up.

TREBUCHET
Trebuchets were used to hurl rocks at a castle's walls to break down its defences. They were also used to throw dead animals over the walls in the hope of spreading disease among the defenders.

CROSSBOW
Crossbows became popular from about 1100. They fired bolts with great force.

MURDER-HOLES
Murderholes could be used to pour boiling water or other unpleasant surprises on to an attacker, or water on to a fire below.

CALTROPS
Caltrops were spiky metal devices that were scattered to slow down the enemy. They could lame horses and foot soldiers.

THE AGE OF INVASIONS

The Middle Ages started with a time of upheaval. The Roman empire was declining in western Europe, and was invaded by one enemy after another. Vandals invaded Spain and Africa; Jutes, Angles and Saxons invaded England; Goths invaded Italy and Gaul. The Romans called these invaders 'barbarians'. Their way of life was warlike, and their leaders were battle heroes. They set up their own kingdoms, fighting for land and power. These invasions of the 3rd, 4th and 5th centuries AD were followed by another wave of invasions from about 800. Three new warlike peoples invaded Europe: Vikings in the north; Arabs in the south; and Hungarians in the east. Roman civilization was at an end and a way of life known as feudalism took its place.

SHIPWRIGHTS

Vikings were expert shipwrights. They built warships, as well as ships for trading and for fishing. They were the first people in northern Europe to build ships with sails and oars.

SHALLOW DRAUGHT

Viking ships were long and narrow, and had shallow draughts – the depth from the bottom of the hull to the waterline – so they could be sailed far upriver.

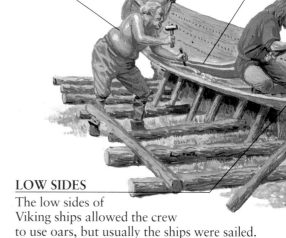

LOW SIDES

The low sides of Viking ships allowed the crew to use oars, but usually the ships were sailed.

LOOK OUT FOR THESE

☐ HELMET

Warriors and leaders were buried with their weapons – their most valued possessions. This helmet was found at the site of the Sutton Hoo burial in England.

☐ VANDAL MOSAIC

This mosaic shows a Vandal, one of the peoples who invaded the Roman empire.

☐ FOOT SOLDIERS

England was invaded by Angles and Saxons who fought on foot, as this painting shows.

VIKING SHIPBUILDING

The prow of a Viking ship was carved from a single piece of timber. The hull was built up with overlapping planks.

1. Backbone of ship (keel) was laid down first

2. Overlapping rows of planks were nailed together to form hull

3. Crossbeams and floor timbers were attached to hull

4. Decking and a socket for the mast were added

PROW

The prow of a Viking ship would often be carved and decorated. Animal or human heads were popular designs.

WORKING WITH TIMBER

Shipwrights used simple tools, like axes, saws and adzes. For the intricate carving on the prow they used chisels, files and gouges.

KING AND COUNCIL

In this Anglo-Saxon painting you can see a king and his advisers. As the invading tribes settled, their leaders became kings, their warriors became nobles, and some of the nobles formed a council to advise the king.

TREASURE

This gold buckle is part of a treasure hoard buried in the 4th century. War leaders rewarded their followers with rich gifts taken from their enemies. Rings, jewellery, gold, silver and weapons were all very important.

FEUDALISM

Feudalism is a word historians use to describe the way of life in the Middle Ages. It comes from a Latin word meaning a grant of land. In a feudal country, the king was not powerful enough to rule by himself. He needed supporters all over the country to help him. He gave land to the lords who promised to support him – such as by fighting in the king's wars – and they, in turn, gave away some of their land to other people. Thus grants of land went from the king right down to the very poorest people on tiny smallholdings. The poor promised to do farm work in exchange for their land. Anyone who had received land and promised support in return was called a vassal.

QUARRELS

When peasants quarrelled with each other, they took their dispute to the lord of the manor's court.

TENANTS

The lord's tenants had to come to his court when he summoned them. They were needed as witnesses in legal cases, as well as for all sorts of other tasks.

 **LOOK OUT FOR THESE**

■ **DOMESDAY BOOK**
The Domesday Book was a great survey made in England for King William the Conqueror in 1086. It recorded almost all the land in the country and showed that since conquering England in 1066, William had given nearly all the land to the Normans.

■ **OATH OF ALLEGIANCE**
A scene from the Bayeux Tapestry shows a tenant swearing to obey the lord whose land he held.

LORD OF THE MANOR

The owner of a manor – an estate in the country – was called the lord of the manor. The lord of the manor had the right to hold a law court for his tenants.

SEISIN

When the lord let a tenant hold land, a special ceremony took place. The tenant was given a clod of earth, which represented the land. This was called 'giving seisin'.

■ CHARLEMAGNE

This bronze statue of the Holy Roman emperor, Charlemagne, who lived from about 742 to 814, is in the Louvre in Paris. Charlemagne gave land to his vassals and expected military support in return.

■ THRONE

A throne was a great sign of authority. Kings, nobles and other important people were allowed to sit while less important people had to stand.

RELIGION

The Middle Ages were very important in the development of religion, for this was the time when paganism died out. Paganism was the belief that there were gods in natural things like the Sun and trees. Three great religions became dominant instead: Christianity, Judaism and Islam (whose followers are called Muslims). Each of these religions teaches that there is only one God. Christianity was the main religion in Europe. Jews from the Holy Land spread to many parts of Europe, but were always a minority. Islam began in the East in 622. Many wars were fought in the name of religion. The most famous were the Crusades – wars between Muslims and Christians in the Holy Land. These began in 1096 and lasted for 200 years.

ROYAL BELIEVER
If the ruler became Christian, his people did, too.

LOOK OUT FOR THESE

ICON
In eastern Europe, monks made beautiful paintings of Christ and the Virgin Mary, or of the saints, on small wooden panels. These paintings were called icons.

JELLING STONES
At Jelling, in Denmark, a 10th century Danish king set up this elaborately carved stone after he made his people Christian.

STONE CROSS
Carved crosses like this were often set up where the Christian message was first preached by missionaries. A church might later be built nearby.

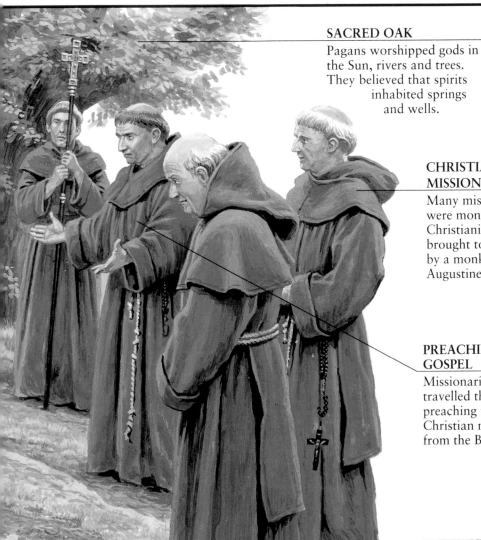

SACRED OAK
Pagans worshipped gods in the Sun, rivers and trees. They believed that spirits inhabited springs and wells.

CHRISTIAN MISSIONARIES
Many missionaries were monks. Christianity was brought to England by a monk called Augustine in 597.

PREACHING THE GOSPEL
Missionaries travelled the country preaching the Christian message from the Bible.

ISLAMIC PRAYER BEADS
Since the Middle Ages, Muslims have used prayer beads like these to help them pray.

ISLAMIC ART
People created especially beautiful places of worship at this time. Islamic artists produced stunning geometric patterns and were particularly skilled at calligraphy, the art of handwriting.

KNIGHTS

Knights were the most important medieval soldiers. Originally a knight was an attendant. But from about 800, knights in the lands of the emperor Charlemagne began to fight on powerful warhorses. Soon fighting on horseback spread to other countries. Only wealthy men could afford to become knights because warhorses were very expensive. So knights were not just important soldiers, they were the important men in the country as well. When a man became a knight, he was 'dubbed', or lightly struck a blow, by his lord, and given his sword.

LADY

Tournaments – competitions between knights – were popular from the 11th century. Many noble women came to watch. Some knights swore to serve one special lady.

HERALDRY

A system of designs on knights' shields identified friends and enemies in battle. This was called heraldry.

 Fleur-de-lis

 Cross

 Bend

 Gyronny

LOOK OUT FOR THESE

SPUR

Warhorses were specially trained to obey their owners' voices, but knights also used spurs like this one to control them. Spurs were worn on the knight's heels. A prick from the spurs urged the horse on.

CHAIN MAIL

Knights needed armour for protection. Some of the first armour was chain mail. It was made from small iron rings linked together to make a knee-length mail shirt.

PLATE ARMOUR

Knights wore full suits of armour from about 1400. It was called 'plate' armour, and was made of steel.

LANCE

The lance was a long pole made of wood. It shattered if it struck a very hard blow.

 SWORD

The sword was the knight's main weapon. Until about 1250, most swords had a double-edged blade, like this one, and a rounded point. Swords with a pointed end for thrusting came later.

RING

A lady might give a knight a ring like this as a sign of her favour.

MONUMENTAL BRASS

Knights' graves were often marked by a brass plate like this, engraved with a picture of the knight in armour.

CASTLES

Castles belonged to kings, nobles and knights – the most important people in the land. A castle was a sign that the owner had power both in times of war and peace. Castles were homes and strong-holds at the same time. They were designed to be difficult for an enemy to attack. The first castles were built in the 9th and 10th centuries, from earth and wood. Designs gradually changed to keep up with new fighting methods.

GREAT TOWER

From the 11th century, great stone towers were built. They were called 'keeps'. Attackers could not burn down a stone keep.

SQUARE CORNERS

Early castles had square corners. But these could be weakened by tunnelling underneath and made the flat walls an easy target to hit with rocks – hence round turrets developed.

NARROW SLIT WINDOWS

Windows were narrow on the outside, to keep out missiles fired by the enemy. Inside, they broadened out to give an archer room to fire on his attackers.

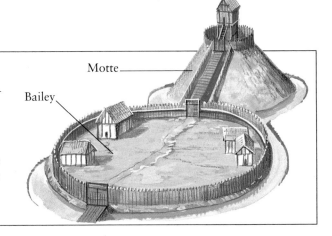

MOTTE AND BAILEY CASTLE

Motte and bailey castles were built in the 11th and 12th centuries. The bailey was an enclosed yard with buildings inside. The motte was a mound of earth with a timber tower on top.

Motte

Bailey

LOOK OUT FOR THESE

■ SPIRAL STAIRCASE

Spiral staircases were designed so that a right-handed invader, fighting his way in, would hit the stonework if he used his sword.

■ TREBUCHET

Trebuchets were used to hurl rocks at a castle's walls to break down its defences. They were also used to throw dead animals over the walls, in the hope of spreading disease among the defenders.

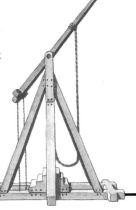

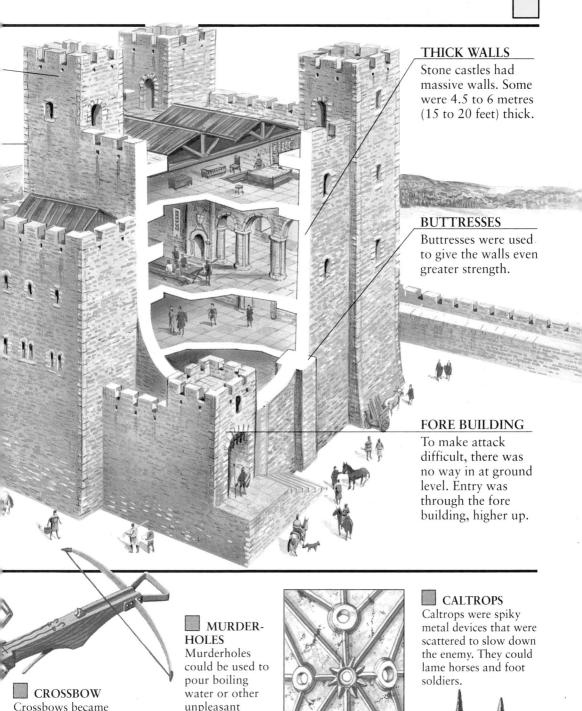

THICK WALLS
Stone castles had massive walls. Some were 4.5 to 6 metres (15 to 20 feet) thick.

BUTTRESSES
Buttresses were used to give the walls even greater strength.

FORE BUILDING
To make attack difficult, there was no way in at ground level. Entry was through the fore building, higher up.

CROSSBOW
Crossbows became popular from about 1100. They fired bolts with great force.

MURDER-HOLES
Murderholes could be used to pour boiling water or other unpleasant surprises on to an attacker, or water on to a fire below.

CALTROPS
Caltrops were spiky metal devices that were scattered to slow down the enemy. They could lame horses and foot soldiers.

WAR

The purpose of a Medieval war was to win land, castles and towns from the enemy. Laying siege to castles and towns was an important way of doing this. Sieges involved bombarding the walls so that the attackers could enter, or trying to starve the inhabitants into surrendering. Europeans learned much about siege warfare from the Arabs during the Crusades. Most wars were fought only during the summer months. Some wars dragged on, like the Hundred Years War (1337–1453) between England and France, in which archers with longbows became important. Medieval wars were supposed to follow a set of rules called the 'law of chivalry'. One rule said that important prisoners were to be ransomed rather than killed. In practice, however, the rules were often ignored.

NORMANS
Normans fought on horseback with swords and lances. They were protected by helmets, coats of chain mail, and shields shaped like kites.

SAXONS
The Saxons rode into battle, but fought on foot. Their main weapons were spears, maces and battle axes.

LOOK OUT FOR THESE

▪ PENNON
The Bayeux Tapestry tells us much about soldiers and weapons at the time of the Battle of Hastings. It shows soldiers carrying spears and lances with an oblong flag or 'pennon' attached. The pennon indicated high rank.

▪ BAGGAGE TRAIN
War was expensive and needed much preparation. The Bayeux Tapestry shows that the Normans had to bring a baggage train of armour, weapons, warhorses and even a castle in kit form with them.

FIGHTING BISHOP
Bishop Odo of Bayeux in Normandy took part in the Battle of Hastings in 1066. He was William the Conqueror's half brother.

SHIELD WALL
King Harold's bodyguards had been trained to make a wall of shields that would stand up to charges by the Norman cavalry at the Battle of Hastings.

STIRRUP
Wearing stirrups helped soldiers keep their balance when fighting on horseback, especially when charging with a lance.

LOOTING
Many medieval pictures show soldiers looting their enemies. They made off with armour, weapons like these, and even sheep and cattle. In the Hundred Years War, some soldiers made fortunes this way.

MACE
The mace was a weapon used by noblemen. Maces were popular in the 1300s because they could injure an enemy even if he was wearing plate armour.

MONASTIC LIFE

Monks and nuns devoted their lives to God. They lived in single-sex communities called monasteries, taking vows to live in poverty and obedience and not to marry. Famous monastery buildings can still be seen at Rievaulx in England and Caen in France, for example. There were different groups of monks and nuns, like the Benedictines, Cistercians and Carthusians, but their basic ways of life were similar. Monastic life began in Egypt in the 3rd century. It quickly became very popular. Saint Benedict, who lived from about 480 to about 546, set a pattern for monastic life, dividing the days and nights into times for work and times for prayer. Benedict's daily timetable is still used in monasteries today.

GUEST HOUSE
Monasteries had a duty to welcome travellers and to provide them with a bed for the night.

CLOISTERS
The monks could take walks, write, read and pray here.

LOOK OUT FOR THESE

TONSURE
Monks had their hair clipped on top. The hairstyle was called a tonsure. This medieval picture shows Guthlac (667-714) being given a tonsure.

PESTLE AND MORTAR
Pestles and mortars were used to pound up herbs to make medicines. Monks and nuns were skilled in making herbal remedies.

CHALICE
Prayer and worship were the most important parts of life for monks and nuns. At the religious service called Mass they used a special cup, or chalice, like this.

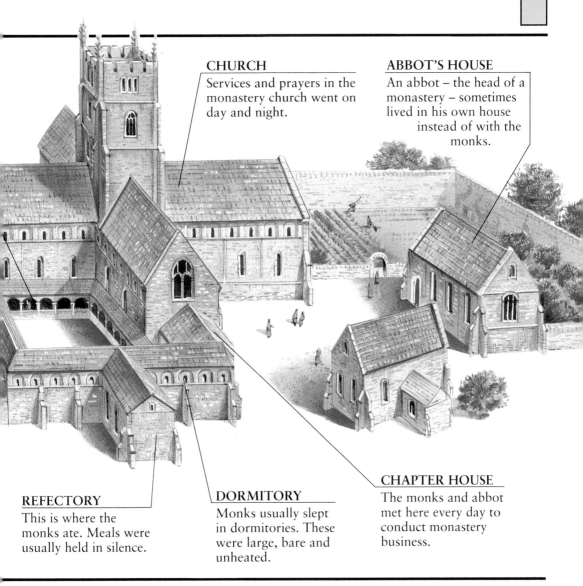

CHURCH
Services and prayers in the monastery church went on day and night.

ABBOT'S HOUSE
An abbot – the head of a monastery – sometimes lived in his own house instead of with the monks.

REFECTORY
This is where the monks ate. Meals were usually held in silence.

DORMITORY
Monks usually slept in dormitories. These were large, bare and unheated.

CHAPTER HOUSE
The monks and abbot met here every day to conduct monastery business.

■ MISERICORD
Misericords were hinged, tip-up seats in the monastery church, often decorated on the underside with carvings like these. Monks and nuns were allowed to lean on the misericords during long services. Misericord means 'mercy'.

■ ROSARY BEADS
Rosary beads were used for prayer. The Dominican friars – who went out preaching – made the rosary very popular.

ART AND ARCHITECTURE

In the Middle Ages, art and architecture were thought of as practical skills. Artists' work was made to be used, not just admired as it often is today. Most art and architecture was created for the Church, to help people pray and think about God; or to make the homes of kings and nobles more splendid and comfortable. For the Church, painters made wall paintings of Bible stories; jewellers and goldsmiths made chalices, shrines and reliquaries (containers for the relics of holy people); sculptors made statues of angels and saints; and architects built soaring churches and cathedrals. For the nobles, artists and craftsmen created tapestries (which were hung on the walls to keep out draughts), tableware, jewellery and highly decorated chests and cupboards.

WORKING WITH STONE

The wheelbarrow was invented in China in the 3rd century and later introduced to Europe. Tread-wheels also lifted stone. The wheel turned as a man walked inside it.

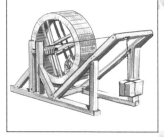

BUILDING CATHEDRALS

Building magnificent churches and cathedrals was widely regarded as a way of praising God.

 LOOK OUT FOR THESE

PAINTED GLASS

Glass windows in glowing colours were made for churches. Some of the finest 12th-century examples can be seen in Chartres Cathedral, in France.

SCULPTURE

Sculptures in churches were not just decorations. They also taught the ordinary people, who could not read, the stories in the Bible. This sculpture shows Jesus appearing to His friends after He rose from the dead.

THINNER WALLS

The Gothic style became important from about 1150. The biggest difference between Gothic and Romanesque churches was that the walls were much thinner – a result of new building technology.

FLYING BUTTRESS

Flying buttresses support the weight of the building. They were a key feature of Gothic architecture. Now walls could be thinner and have larger windows.

MORTAR

Mortar was made from sand and lime. It was applied to stone with trowels similar to those used today.

◼ MASON'S MARK

Masons put identifying marks on the stones they cut. This was because they were usually paid according to how much work they did.

◼ TOOLS

The tools used by masons and sculptors were similar to tools used today: hammers, chisels, axes, saws, set squares, punches and gouges.

◼ ROMANESQUE

Romanesque buildings, based on the style of ancient Rome, belong to the early Middle Ages. Churches from this period, like Durham Cathedral in England, have thick walls and huge pillars supporting vaulted roofs.

LEARNING

Few people could read or write in the Middle Ages. Merchants and tradespeople taught themselves arithmetic and learned to keep their business accounts. The children of noble families learned to read at home. But it was the men who served God in the Church – as priests, monks, friars, bishops and abbots – who were the best educated people at the time. They learned Latin, which was the language of the Bible, of Church services, and of many official government documents. Schools were set up in some monasteries and cathedrals, and universities such as Paris and Oxford were started. Here, too, religious studies were considered the most important subjects, but there was growing interest in medicine as well.

SCRIPTORIUM
Part of the monastery cloisters was set aside for writing. This area was called the 'scriptorium'.

QUILL PEN
Pens were made from bird feathers. Quills from a goose or swan were best. The pen tip wore down with use and had to be sharpened with a 'pen knife'.

1. Quill from bird

2. Stripped down and tip angled to form nib

LOOK OUT FOR THESE

COLOURS
In manuscripts, capital letters were often decorated. Fine beaten gold, called gold leaf, was used. Some colours were made from plant juices.

CHARTER AND SEALS
Charters were official documents. They recorded events such as grants of land, when towns were founded and decisions in law cases. A seal proved that the charter was genuine.

PARCHMENT

Books and documents were written on material called parchment, which was made from animal skin.

ILLUMINATED MANUSCRIPT

Medieval books were decorated with beautiful coloured pictures. They are called 'illuminated manuscripts' because they seem to glow with colour (illuminated) and were written by hand (manuscript).

BOOKS

Because books were written by hand – and only a few people could write – they were rare and treated with great respect. Most books were on religious subjects and were written by monks.

LINDISFARNE GOSPEL

This is a page from a Gospel book written at the monastery on Lindisfarne, an island off the English coast, in about 700. For medieval monks, copying out the Scriptures was a way of worshipping God.

OAK APPLE

Ink, for use with quill pens, could be made from acid and iron gall, a substance found in a growth on oak trees called a 'gall' or oak apple.

STYLUS

Before a writer began work, he ruled guide lines for his writing on the parchment. This was done by scoring it with a stylus like this. A stylus had a metal tip and was made from bone.

PEASANTS

The poorest medieval people were the peasants. They lived in the countryside, which they farmed. The very poorest peasants, called 'villeins', were not free. They belonged to the lord of the manor and he could sell or give them to someone else if he wanted. They could not educate their sons, or marry off their daughters, or move away from the place where they lived without their lord's permission. They were allowed to grow their own food on a plot of land owned by the lord of the manor, and in return for this they had to work for the lord and farm his fields as well. Farmwork included shearing the sheep, weeding the corn, loading the hay on to carts, mending tools and collecting honey.

FOOD

The lord of the manor usually provided food for his peasants at harvest time.

THRESHING

Threshing was the last job of the harvest. The corn was beaten with a tool called a flail, which separated the grain from the husk and straw.

 **LOOK OUT FOR THESE**

JOHN BALL

John Ball, seen here in a drawing from a medieval chronicle (record of events), was one of the leaders of a rebellion called the Peasants' Revolt. It started in England in 1381. John Ball wanted freedom and justice for the poor.

MANOR HOUSE

The lord of the manor lived in a house, like this 14th-century manor house. His peasants provided food for the household. Sometimes they had to give him some of their crops and animals.

OPEN FIELDS

Strips of land belonging to one peasant were scattered in different parts of two or three enormous fields. They were not fenced off from everyone else's.

WOMEN

Peasant women had to toil on the land as well as looking after home and family.

HARVESTING

Cutting the corn was a job the peasants all did together. The lord's corn always had to be cut first.

▨ PLOUGH

Ploughs turned the soil over to make the fields ready for crops to be sown. They were pulled by a team of eight oxen.

▨ RARE BREED

Many sheep were kept in large parts of England and Spain. Some breeds that were very common in the Middle Ages, like this one, are rare today, but can still be seen on special 'rare breeds' farms.

COUNTRY LIFE

Most medieval people lived in small village communities in the countryside. Towns were very rare. Country life followed a regular pattern every year. In spring the fields were ploughed, the crops were sown and the sheep were lambed and sheared. In summer the crops were weeded and manured, and hay was made. In autumn came the harvest, and in winter wood had to be cut for fuel and many other jobs had to be done. Each village or manor was more or less self sufficient. There would be local craftsmen like blacksmiths to make scythes, parts for the plough and other farm tools people needed. The local parish church was the centre of village life.

THATCHING

A thatcher was a craftsman who thatched roofs. Thatch was made from bundles of reeds.

ANIMALS

Peasants often shared their cottages with their animals. Chickens roosted on the rafters, and there was sometimes a byre or shed for a cow.

LOOK OUT FOR THESE

■ LABOURS OF THE MONTHS

Church carvings often showed peasants doing their monthly tasks. This one shows a man carrying hay in August.

■ FOREST SCENE

Keeping pigs was an important part of village life. In autumn the pigs were fattened up, often on acorns and nuts. This picture is from a medieval prayer book. Prayer books often contained scenes of everyday life.

WINDMILL

Each village had its own mill where corn was ground into flour. Windmills came to Europe from the East in about 1150.

COTTAGES

Villagers built their own cottages. Great beams of wood supported the side walls. Windows did not have glass, just wooden shutters to keep out draughts.

PARISH PRIEST

The priest baptized and sometimes taught village children, buried the dead and performed marriage ceremonies.

STOCKS

People who broke the law were often put in the stocks as a punishment. Passers-by could pelt them with sticks, stones and rotten vegetables.

SHEPHERDS

This cathedral sculpture shows shepherds and their sheep. Spain was famous for its sheep in the Middle Ages. It had 1 million in 1360.

SCYTHE

Sickles and scythes were used for cutting crops. Harvests were smaller than they are today, partly because little fertilizer was used.

PIG STICKING

This prayer-book picture of country life shows a pig being killed to provide food for winter – a gruesome but important autumn job. Many animals were killed at this time of year.

TOWNS AND CRAFTS

From the 11th century, towns grew up in many parts of Europe. Some of these were completely new. Places like Villeneuve, which means 'new town' in French, date back to this time. Towns were the homes of specialist craftsmen and traders such as grocers, spicers, cobblers, apothecaries and goldsmiths. These craftsmen joined together into societies called guilds. The guilds made rules about prices and wages. They had a social side, too. Members met for feasts and for special religious services. In big towns, all the shops of one kind tended to group together. In Florence, in Italy, the goldsmiths' shops were on a bridge called the Ponte Vecchio, for example.

APPRENTICES
Children trained to become craftsmen by working as apprentices to master craftsmen, who were paid to take them on.

LOOK OUT FOR THESE

ITALIAN TOWNS
Italian towns were the wealthiest and most famous of all medieval towns. Townspeople liked to build fine buildings as a sign of their town's greatness. The leaning tower of Pisa, begun in 1173, was one of these.

CHURCH WINDOW
Guilds often paid for church windows – like this one showing a member of the drapers' guild.

TOWN WALLS
Towns had walls for protection, as this seal shows. The gates were shut at night so no-one could go in or out.

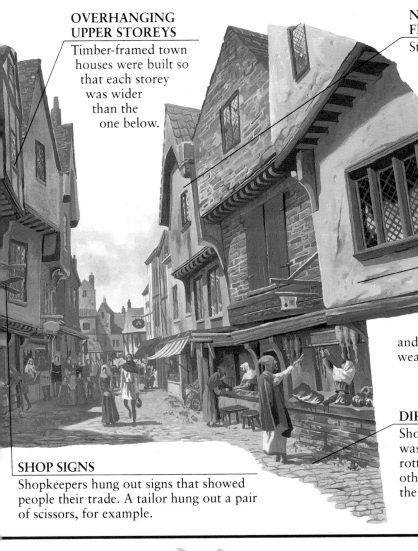

OVERHANGING UPPER STOREYS

Timber-framed town houses were built so that each storey was wider than the one below.

NARROW HOUSE FRONTS

Street frontage was expensive, so town houses and shops tended to be deep and narrow, with the narrow end facing on to the street.

BUILDING MATERIALS

Most houses were made of wood and plaster. Stone houses were rare and usually only built by wealthy people.

DIRTY STREETS

Shopkeepers threw their waste (scraps, offal, rotten vegetables and other rubbish) out on to the street.

SHOP SIGNS

Shopkeepers hung out signs that showed people their trade. A tailor hung out a pair of scissors, for example.

LOOM

Cloth making was an important medieval craft. Wool was made into cloth by weavers who used looms like this one. This type of loom was first used in Europe in about the 13th century.

SCALES

Goldsmiths made jewellery, fine tableware and many other precious objects. Their guilds carefully regulated their work by weighing the gold and jewels on scales like these.

TRADE

Fairs were centres for long-distance trade. Here merchants from all over Europe and the East gathered to buy and sell their wares. The most famous fairs were held in Champagne in France every year. There was a twelve-day cloth fair, an eight-day leather fair, and fairs for other goods as well. Italy was also an important trading country because of its key position between Europe and the East. Merchants from Venice traded with the Byzantine empire through the port of Constantinople (modern Istanbul in Turkey), and merchants from Pisa and Genoa traded with the Muslim cities of North Africa. As trade increased around the world, so did the development of banks and accounting.

BANK
Banks grew up to help merchants from different countries pay each other.

BUYING IN BULK
Large households sent their servants to fairs to buy a whole year's supply of items such as salt or cloth that could not be bought nearer home.

SHEEP TRADE
Sheep were sometimes driven long distances to market. The Lendit fair, held at Saint Denis in France in June each year, drew shepherds from all over the surrounding countryside.

 **LOOK OUT FOR THESE**

SPICES
Spicy food was very popular. Spices like these cinnamon sticks and cloves were brought to Europe from India and other Eastern countries. The spice trade created great riches for the merchants involved.

COINS
Coins were made from gold or silver. In Italy there was a gold coin called a florin, and in France there was one called an ecu.

LAPIS LAZULI
The best shade of blue for painters came from the lapis lazuli stone, shown here as powder in an oyster shell dish. Rare and expensive, the stones came from mines in Central Asia.

MERCHANT

A merchant's main aim was to make money. Many people, especially the nobility, thought this was not a respectable way to live.

PACK ANIMAL

Goods were carried by pack animals such as mules, and in carts. Merchants travelled together as protection against robbers.

MERCHANT'S MARK

Merchants had their own 'mark' or design to identify the owner of goods sent to fairs and markets. Their mark was often cut on to a ring like this. Pressed into melted wax, it could be used as a seal.

SILK

Silk like this was worn by wealthy people. The Italian towns of Florence, Venice and Lucca were great silk-weaving centres. Merchants also bought silk called baldachin in Baghdad and fine cloth called damask in Damascus to sell in Europe.

TRAVEL AND EXPLORATION

Few people travelled far from home. The world beyond Europe was a great mystery, said to contain animals like the mythical 'centicore' – a cross between a horse and a lion, with the voice of a man. But fact began to replace fantasy as travellers and merchants made longer and longer voyages on business. Marco Polo (1254–1324), a merchant from Venice, was especially famous for his travels. He journeyed as far as the court of Kublai Khan in China. A man who travelled even further than Marco Polo was Ibn Battuta (1304–1369) from Morocco. He visited south-east Asia, China and many Muslim countries.

SEA FIGHT
Sailors had to defend themselves with weapons if their ship was attacked. They used the same weapons as soldiers on land.

RUDDER
Rudders were invented at the end of the 13th century. They were used for steering.

LOOK OUT FOR THESE

ASTROLABE
From the 15th century, astrolabes were used to measure the angle of the stars above the horizon as a way of navigating. The best ones were made by the Muslims in the East and in Spain.

CART
Many medieval pictures show carts like this one. Peasants rode in carts, and prisoners were taken to their execution in them.

MAP
This map was drawn in the 1100s. The map-maker thought the world was a circle divided into four.

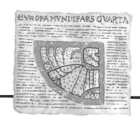

EVROPA MVNDI PARS QVARTA

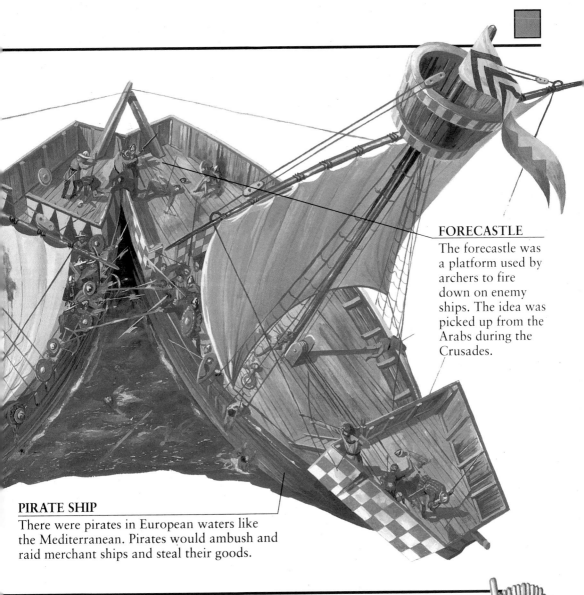

FORECASTLE

The forecastle was a platform used by archers to fire down on enemy ships. The idea was picked up from the Arabs during the Crusades.

PIRATE SHIP

There were pirates in European waters like the Mediterranean. Pirates would ambush and raid merchant ships and steal their goods.

LITTER

Wealthy women travelled in horse-drawn litters like the one shown in this picture from a medieval manuscript. Nobles travelled more than poor people, visiting their many estates. Their families and servants travelled with them.

CREEL

Creels were made from straw or wicker. They were carried on the back and used for heavy loads. They were used in some countries until quite recent times.

ENTERTAINMENT AND HOLY DAYS

Our word 'holiday' comes from the Middle Ages. Then, it meant 'holy day', a special religious feast day when work stopped. There were about 40 to 50 holy days during the year. People were expected to go to three church services each holy day, and to fast the night before! But there were plenty of other ways to fill the time. There were entertainers such as jugglers and acrobats. In towns there were processions and plays about Bible stories, such as Noah and the Ark. Some people liked to gamble with dice and to play cards.

TROUBADOUR

Troubadours were wandering minstrels. They sang songs, played music and told stories. Especially popular were tales of knights and their ladies, full of heroism and romance.

PUPPET SHOW

Entertainers such as puppeteers travelled from place to place. They gave performances at castles and manor houses, in villages and at fairs.

LOOK OUT FOR THESE

■ SAINT JAMES OF COMPOSTELA

Many pilgrims prayed at the tomb of Saint James of Compostela in Spain. Pilgrimages were religious occasions, but they were also holidays from work.

■ PILGRIM BADGE

People could buy special badges to show where they had been on pilgrimage and to which saints they were devoted. This badge shows Saint Catherine, who was put to death on a wheel.

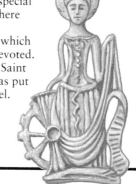

HOUSEHOLD ANIMALS

Many people kept animals such as dogs and cats. More extraordinary pets were monkeys, jays and magpies. Some kings kept lions and other wild animals.

DANCING BEAR

Some entertainers travelled with performing animals. Bears were trained to dance and apes to do somersaults. Some entertainments were cruel, like setting dogs to fight bears.

BIRD OF PREY

Hunting with birds of prey such as falcons was a popular pastime for the nobility.

CHESSMAN

Chess was popular with the nobility. Bets were often placed on who would win.

HORNPIPE

Music and dancing were favourite pastimes. A typical instrument was the hornpipe – a wooden pipe joined to a cow's horn.

HOMES AND FAMILIES

Parents were very strict. The father was the head of the family. He took important decisions such as whom his children would marry. A woman had to follow her husband's and father's wishes. If her father died, an heiress would be married off by the nobleman whose land she held. A nobleman's sons were sent away at about the age of seven to become pages in other noble houses, where they learned to be obedient and how to use weapons. Girls learned music, cooking, embroidery and how to manage the household servants.

PAINTED WALLS
Castle walls were decorated with coloured patterns.

SPINNING
Even in wealthy households, girls learned how to weave and spin so that they could make clothes.

BABY-WALKER
Carvings show that some children learned to walk using baby-walkers just as they do today.

✓ **LOOK OUT FOR THESE**

TAPESTRY
Tapestries were used as wall coverings in the homes of rich people. This one shows a noble-woman out hunting. It was made in Arras in Flanders in about 1420.

CHEST
Wooden chests were used for storing linen, clothes, tapestries, jewellery and other goods. They doubled as trunks for carrying belongings when nobles went travelling.

BATH TUB

A half barrel made a good bath tub. It was filled with warm water from a jug.

FIRE

Not all rooms were heated, but those that were had roaring log fires.

RUSH FLOORING

Rushes and herbs were put down as floor covering.

PRICKET CANDLESTICK

Pricket candlesticks had a long spike to hold the candle in place. Candles were used to light churches and rich people's homes.

WATTLE AND DAUB

Wattle and daub was a cheap building material. Wattle was a weave of twigs and daub was a coating of mud and straw plastered on top.

CAPUCHIN

This style of head-dress is a 'capuchin'. Part of it was pulled round the shoulders like a cape, and the rest formed a hood. Capuchins were worn until about 1500.

FOOD AND DRINK

Poor people mostly ate vegetables such as beans and cabbage, and coarse oatmeal bread, eggs, cheese and bacon. They drank milk or ale. Rich people had a more varied diet. Hunting provided meat for their tables, especially venison. They ate white bread, drank wine, and used spices and rich sauces to hide the taste of food that was going off. Feasts were great social occasions for the rich. The sons of knights served at feasts, carving the meat and pouring water for guests to wash their hands. Books were written describing good table manners. They advised people not to scratch, put their elbows on the table, or pick their teeth during meals.

COOKING ON A SPIT
Meat was roasted on a spit in great households, or cut up and boiled in a cauldron. The spit was turned slowly during cooking.

WINE

The best wine came from France and Italy. It was transported and kept in wooden casks, but there was always a danger that it would turn sour when brought long distances.

 LOOK OUT FOR THESE

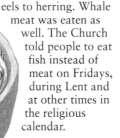

 FISH
All kinds of fish ended up on the table, from eels to herring. Whale meat was eaten as well. The Church told people to eat fish instead of meat on Fridays, during Lent and at other times in the religious calendar.

KNIVES
Knives were valued possessions. Men usually wore one on their belt for use while out hunting, as well as for eating. The knives shown here are too elegant for rough use, and would have been kept for the table. Forks were used from about 1400.

PRESERVING FOOD

There were several ways to preserve food. Fish could be dried, meat salted, and hams smoked near the fire.

WASHING UP

Water had to be brought from a well and carried indoors. Metal cups and dishes were boiled in bran and rubbed with a cloth.

AQUAMANILE

Guests washed in scented water brought in splendid water jugs like this one, called aquamaniles.

BEE HIVE

Honey, not sugar, was the usual sweetener, and bee hives were a common sight. Hives like this one were made of straw. Wooden bee boxes were also used. Hives and boxes can be seen in many medieval manuscripts.

GARDEN PRODUCE

Gardens were not just kept for pleasure. Fruit, vegetables, nuts, herbs and flowers provided food and homemade medicines.

CHANGE AND DISCOVERY

The Middle Ages did not finish on one particular day, but from about 1400 ideas began to change, especially about religion. There were also new inventions, such as gunpowder and cannons, which turned castles and knights on horseback into things of the past. Deadly plagues hit Europe from 1348, killing about a third of the people. With fewer people to work the land, the peasants could demand better conditions. All these changes meant that the medieval, feudal way of life was coming to an end. Explorers from Spain and Portugal, such as Bartholomew Diaz (c.1450–1500) and Christopher Columbus (1451–1506), discovered new lands and opened up the world.

BREACH IN THE WALL
Castles no longer made good strongholds once cannons were developed that could severely damage walls and even blow holes in them.

LOOK OUT FOR THESE

PRINTING PRESS
Johannes Gutenberg invented the printing press in 1453. Presses like this were soon widely used in Europe. Books no longer had to be written by hand.

LIFELIKE ART
This statue, by the sculptor Verrocchio, is of a great Italian soldier, Bartolomeo Colleoni, who died in 1476. It is an example of the new lifelike style of art that began to develop about 1400.

GUNPOWDER

Gunpowder, which was invented in China, was first used in Europe in about 1250. It was made from sulphur, charcoal and saltpetre. The first weapons to cause explosions did not work very well.

BATTERING RAM

Old ways of fighting, such as using battering rams, carried on alongside the new cannons.

CANNON

Cannons of different sizes were used from about 1320. They fired stone (and later metal) balls.

CARAVEL

In the 1400s sailors from Spain and Portugal developed a type of ship called the caravel to withstand rough seas.

PLAGUE ATTACK

People feared the pain of plague. They likened it to being shot with arrows, as shown in the scene on this woodcut.

RELICS

In medieval times people often prayed near saints' relics. This reliquary or casket held the relics of Saint Faith. But as ideas changed, some relics and reliquaries were destroyed.

Glossary

Words in SMALL CAPITAL letters indicate a cross-reference.

abbey A MONASTERY.

abbot MONK in charge of an ABBEY.

apothecary Someone who mixes and sells medicines, making them out of herbs and other ingredients.

apprentice Boy or girl learning a trade or craft from a master craftsman.

astrolabe Instrument for studying the stars and plotting the course of a ship at sea.

Benedictines MONKS and NUNS who followed the way of life set out by Saint Benedict.

bishop The top church leader in an area. His church is a CATHEDRAL.

Byzantine empire Part of the Roman empire that survived in eastern Europe after the part centred on Rome was conquered. Its capital was Constantinople.

Carthusians MONKS who lived a solitary, silent way of life. The order was started in the late 1000s.

castle A stronghold. Also the home of a KNIGHT or NOBLE.

cathedral The most important church in a particular area.

chalice Special cup used at CHRISTIAN religious services.

Christian Someone who believes that Jesus is the Son of God.

chronicle Written account of events by someone who lived at the time.

Cistercians Group of MONKS and NUNS – started in the late 1000s – who wanted to live a more simple way of life than the BENEDICTINES.

Crusades Wars fought between CHRISTIANS and MUSLIMS in the HOLY LAND.

draper Someone who sells cloth.

feudalism Society where the people who own land have power over the people who live on it.

friar Man who gave up all his possessions and went out teaching people about God.

goldsmith Craftsman who worked with gold and jewels.

Gospel book A book containing the part of the Bible that tells the story of Jesus Christ.

Gothic Style of building used for churches from about 1100.

guild Group of craftsmen or merchants.

Holy Land Parts of the Middle East described in the Bible and the Qur'an, the Holy Book of Islam.

illuminated manuscript Text written by hand, with beautifully coloured illustrations.

keep Great stone tower forming part of a CASTLE.

knight Important soldier who fought on horseback.

Latin Language spoken by the Romans. It was still used in the Middle Ages for Church services, the Bible and documents.

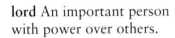

lord An important person with power over others.

lord of the manor Person who owned a MANOR.

manor Big farm in the country owned by a KNIGHT or NOBLE.

missionary Someone who travels to foreign lands to tell people about God.

monastery Place where MONKS live.

monk Man who takes special religious vows to serve God, and lives in a MONASTERY.

Muslim Someone who follows the teaching of the prophet Muhammad and the Islamic religion.

noble Rich and important person.

Normans People from Normandy in France. The Normans conquered England in 1066.

nun Woman who takes special religious vows to serve God, and lives in a house with other nuns.

peasant Poor person who lives by farming.

pilgrim Person who goes on a PILGRIMAGE.

pilgrimage Journey to pray at a great church or the SHRINE of a SAINT.

priest Person in charge of a local church, who takes religious services and teaches the local people about God.

psalms Prayers that form part of the Bible.

psalter A book of PSALMS.

relic Something that once belonged to a SAINT. It may be remains of the saint's clothes, hair, bones or teeth.

reliquary Special casket in which a RELIC is kept.

Romanesque Style of building that was used for churches from about 900.

rosary Prayer beads.

saint An especially holy person, believed by many to be able to work miracles because of their faith in God.

Saxons People who lived in England at the time of the NORMAN Conquest.

seisin Occupying a piece of land.

shipwright Person who makes ships.

shrine Holy place where the RELICS of a SAINT are kept.

stocks Wooden construction that held a prisoner's hands or feet. Passers-by would throw things at the person.

tapestry Large, decorative piece of needlework made to hang on the wall of a rich person's house.

tenant Person who holds and rents a piece of land from another.

tonsure Clipped haircut worn by MONKS.

tournament Mock battle held between KNIGHTS. Tournaments were very popular, and crowds flocked to watch.

vassal Someone who swore to be loyal to a more powerful person.

villein Poorest sort of PEASANT in the Middle Ages, whose freedom was very limited.

INDEX